Future And Options Trading Stratergies

Guide to Indian Share Market

by PB EPUBLISHER

Published by:

PB EPUBLISHER

©Copyright 2016 – PB EPUBLISHER

ISBN-13: 978-1540367914
ISBN-10: 1540367916

Table of Contents

Chapter 1: Introduction to Future and Options

The futures and options has been an area of keen interest to the investors over a long period of time. The flexibility they provide is unmatchable. With the ever changing market and the experiences of cyclic volatile phases, many of the investors consider them to be lucrative as well as profitable. But to get into the depths of this discipline we must understand the basic terminology of derivatives and the trade involving these options. Let us begin from the ground level of this subject. The market is not made of one man.

There are number of traders and investors that collectively form a market. Now, you cannot expect every trader to carry the same perspective as you do. With people, there is always a conflict of views. Imagine a market where everyone is rushing into a conflict over the prices of the stocks. Some would say that they will rise in the future and the others would be negative to the rise of prices. The feature of the market that we trade in is that it allows the complete flow of information without any hindrance. This allows us to trade freely and totally on our instincts. With all the shared knowledge that we receive as investors is the way to know about the market behavior that ultimately designs our strategy. Accordingly, we decide to take our positions which may be bullish or bearish depending completely on the future price of the stocks. Now what we are dealing here in is called the derivative market. We here have two things that give us the definition of derivatives and these are – assets and value. The shares are the 'assets'. The shares we hold or the so called assets we hold give 'value' to the derivatives. And the most common derivatives we deal with in the market are – the futures and options. There are others also such as warrants and convertible bonds but we are concerned with the former ones in this book. These are basically financial instruments. The asset cannot just be a stock but also the bonds, commodities, currencies, interest rates and market indexes. When you are dealing with these derivatives, what you is that you place a bet or set a contract on whether the value of your asset will increase or decrease within a period of time. Henceforth, these derivatives are supposed to get their value from the existing or future prices of the underlying security. Here is one interesting thing to know. When you are dealing with the derivatives, you are essentially receiving the ownership of the asset rather than the asset itself from the original owner. This is an important trait of this method that allows flexibility as well as attracts the investors. The options contract will give you the power to either buy or sell the asset on or before a given date at a pre-set price whereas the futures contract is a legal agreement on the buying or selling of an asset on the end date of the contract or famously called the expiry date. We will discuss each one of the two in detail later through the length of this book. The whole of the derivative market deals with speculations so not expecting a risk would be a lie to your true self. By now we are quite familiar with these two terms – the first one is 'underlying' and the second one is 'contracts'. The 'underlying' is the spot price of the market and the 'contracts' is devoted to a specific traded instrument in the derivative market. We have three different participants in the market

Speculators: They undertake high risks in the market. These participants are known to bet on the future movement of the prices according to their knowledge and skill in taking higher risks to produce profits which are quantitatively higher than average levels. They work out in the market by two strategies- buy low and sell high or sell high and buy low.

Hedgers: They trade in range and watch the market activity closely. They take risks but up to a certain level. A hedger would protect himself by selling the stock as soon as it reaches the optimum price assuring a certain amount of profit to him. They are always looking for factors to reduce risk for their holdings and stocks. They are important to a market as they are responsible to set future prices of the stocks.

Arbitrageur: The arbitrageurs are the most experienced players of the market that make fast and rational decisions. They are known to make offset transactions to profit from the inefficiencies in the price. The source of their profit is the way they buy low in one market and sell high in the other. They are responsible for the stability of the market prices thus reduce the exploitation of the prices.

So, it can be concluded that if you are going to deal in the futures and options which basically means you are involved in the derivatives market, there are these three things that you should be clear in your mind. The first one is that you are going to trade on the price movements of the market. The second one is always expect risk and uncertainties in this market. And, the last one is that you are going to make profits from the short term mispricing. The methods as futures and options are a way to redistribute the risk generated by different economies of the world be it a global one or some domestic economy. They protect the assets from running undervalued or overvalued by regulating the pricing of these. Let us now understand the basics of futures and options. These two are the instruments that give flexibility to the derivative market.

Chapter 2: UNDERSTANDING THE 'FUTURES' & PLANNING STRATEGIES

As mentioned earlier, it is a derivative instrument that involves two parties who make an agreement for the transaction of an asset or may be physical commodities that will be delivered in the future at a particular price. It can be understood as essentially agreeing to buy something that has not been produced yet and that too for a set price. One important thing to note here is that when you are involved in the futures market, you do not compulsorily have to be responsible for receiving or delivering large amounts of physical commodities but it is more like hedging risk or speculating rather than involving in the exchange of physical commodities. That is the primary reason behind referring the futures market as a financial instrument that is used by not only the producers and consumers but also by the speculators. It provides an intense competition between the buyers and the sellers. It is majorly known to work as a hub for managing financial risks. The complexity of its nature includes risk and extreme fluidity which need some high efforts to understand. Now to understand this completely, let us take an example. The future market as the name states is the one that is dealt in future but the details are set presently. Imagine a farmer who produces wheat every year. The other person involved in this scenario is the bread maker.

The farmer and the bread maker run into an agreement that states the delivery and the receiving of a particular amount of wheat in the future at a pre determined price. No matter where the price value goes in the future, it is the contract that binds the two to stick to the price that has been already decided. This ensures the profitability of the both parties. The price value is decided before the contract binding that is considered fair by both the parties. Henceforth, it is the contract that is sold in the futures market and not the grain itself which justifies the earlier statement of the futures market that states- The futures market does not necessarily involve the exchange of the physical asset but it is the contract that is sold. This market can be considered as a centralized marketplace for both the buyers and sellers where they can enter into futures contract. Either an open cry system or bids can be the basis of pricing. The offers are matched electronically and the price will be paid on the date of the delivery.

The two parties involved in the contract are categorized as a short position (the party who delivers or agrees to deliver a commodity) and a long position (the party who receives or agrees to receive a commodity). This will discussed later on in the book. An important characteristic of this contract is that everything involved in the agreement is already specified, both in terms of quality as well as quantity. The price per unit and the date of delivery are covered under the contract. The profits and losses are decided by the daily movements of the stock market and are calculated on a daily basis. Now it is not the value of the price that differs but the profit and loss statement which is influenced by the normal market prices at the time of delivery. The payable price will always remain the same as mentioned in the contract. Let us understand this with an example. As an obliged seller of wheat, you will have to deliver it at the rates mentioned in the contract. Suppose the market price of the wheat shifts to Rs. 250 per bushel but you are bounded to deliver at Rs. 200. This is where the profit and loss of a contract is decided. You are obviously at a loss of Rs. 50 per bushel but the receiver is sure at profit of Rs. 50 per bushel. Hence it can be made out of the above context that the gains and losses are deducted or credited into a person's account each day. As these contracts are adjusted everyday in relation to the account settlements, most transactions of the futures market are made in cash. You can think of it as a parallel movement of the price and the futures market. As soon as the contract expires, this whole bunch of prices merges into one price and henceforth, the contract will be settled.

Let us understand what a 'hedge' means in the futures market. After the contract is settled, the bread maker did not receive any wheat. He still needs to buy wheat to make bread and similarly, the farmer is still left with his wheat in the storage. Both of them will now actually make a buy and a sell in the cash market. The bread maker will buy the bushels for Rs. 250 and the farmer will sell his bushels for Rs. 250. The money earned by the bread maker in the futures market goes into his purchase and the farmer's loss in the futures market also gets filled by the higher selling price in the cash market. This is known as hedging. When we compare this simple example to the speculators, the short peculator would be at a loss whereas the long speculator would gain profit from his position at the expiry of the contract.

As a participant of futures market you will realize that it is highly active and a centre to global market place. It is an indicator of the sentimental positioning of the market. On the economic front of our discussion it can be considered as a major importance holder to the country. The competitiveness of its nature determines it as a significant economic tool that regulates the prices based on the estimated amount of supply and demand of each day. So, it is the hub of market information. The futures market is greatly affected by the socio-economic factors such as war, debt, refugee displacement or land reclamation. The transparency is a necessity to such a market with this much amount of continuous flow of information. It is the way of the people to absorb this information that decides the changes in the prices of a commodity.

This is also usually referred to as price discovery. The risk reduction is the favorite part of futures market. Because the price is pre-set, the risk is eliminated to a certain extent.

We have two participants in the futures market. The first one is the hedgers and the second one is the speculators. The hedgers can be farmers, manufacturers or exporters who buy or sell in the futures market to secure the price of a commodity. They intend to protect themselves from the price risks. The price volatility in the market comes with risk associated to it. The futures market provides a sense of security to both the parties involved in the contract. A long position holder in the futures market will try to bargain a price as low as possible unlike a short position holder who will try to secure as high a price as possible.

The speculators are the participants that aim to benefit from the futures market irrespective of the fact that the market is inherently risky is nature. They do not focus on the minimization of the risk but rather focus on the development of the profits. This is the difference between the hedgers and the speculators. The hedgers want to reduce the risk in whatever they are investing while the speculators want to maximize their profits even on the cost of increased risk. The hedgers and the speculators can be interconnected in few terms. For example, a speculator would buy a contract low in price to sell it high in price in the future and most probably he would be buying that contract from a hedger who is selling it at low prices due to the risk involved in the speculated decline in the prices of the future. So they can be considered as benefiting from each other.

Earlier in this book, two position were mentioned – the long one and the short one. Let us discuss them in detail.

THE LONG POSITION

The long futures position is all about unlimited profit as well as unlimited risk. A speculator is the participant usually involved in this position of the futures market who profits from the **rise in the price** of the underlying. For the initial margin requirement, the trader in the long term position must have enough balance in his account for each futures contract that he is interested in **buying**. There is a maintenance balance that must be always retained in the account to stay in the long futures position. It is required because each day's gains and losses are credited and debited into your account respectively at the end of the trading day. So you do not want a margin account to be set. A trader can stand in the long futures position for as long as the market is rising. So, there is no maximum profit that is linked to the long term futures position. There are calculations available to determine the profit from this position. As the maximum profit is equal to the unlimited and the condition of profit is the greater value of market price of futures than the purchase price of them, the formula for the calculation comes out to be:

- Profit = (Market price – purchase price) * Contract size

Similarly the unlimited risk can also be calculated which is commonly referred to as the loss involved.

The losses mainly occur with a drastic **fall** in the underlying futures price. Here, the maximum loss is equal to the unlimited and the condition of loss has to be the greater value of the purchase price of the futures than the market price of them. Therefore, the formula is as:

- Loss = (Purchase price of the futures – market price of the futures) * contract size + commissions paid

The break-even points are the reference points which signify that the total cost and the total revenue are equal. This means that there is no loss or gain involved in the results of the contract. It can also be calculated and the formula stands as below:

- Breakeven point = purchase price of the futures contract

THE SHORT POSITION

The short term futures position also includes unlimited profit as well as unlimited risk. A speculator is the participant usually involved in this position of the futures market who profits from the **fall in the price** of the underlying. For the initial margin requirement, the trader in the short term position must have enough balance in his account for each futures contract that he is interested in **selling**. There is a maintenance balance that must be always retained in the account to stay in the short futures position. It is required because each day's gains and losses are credited and debited into your account respectively at the end of the trading day. So you do not want a margin account to be set. A trader can stand in the short futures position for as long as the market is declining. So, there is no maximum profit that is linked to the short term futures position. There are calculations available to determine the profit from this position. As the maximum profit is equal to the unlimited and the condition of profit is the lower value of market price of futures than the selling price of them, the formula for the calculation comes out to be:

- Profit = (selling price of the futures − market price of the futures) * Contract size

Similarly the unlimited risk can also be calculated which is commonly referred to as the loss involved. The losses mainly occur with a drastic **rise** in the underlying futures price. Here, the maximum loss is equal to the unlimited and the condition of loss has to be the lesser value of the purchase price of the futures than the market price of them. Therefore, the formula is as:

- Loss = (market price of the futures − selling price of the futures) * contract size + commissions paid

The break-even points are the reference points which signify that the total cost and the total revenue are equal. This means that there is no loss or gain involved in the results of the contract. It can also be calculated for the short term positions and the formula stands as below:

- Breakeven point = selling price of the futures contract

Let us understand some important terms of the futures market:

We mentioned a term 'margin' a few paragraphs back. Here the 'margin' is not same as the one used in the stock market. There the definition turns out to be the borrowed money which is used to purchase securities whereas in the futures market it is completely of a different sense. The margin is the initial deposit of money that is put into an account in order to start in the futures contract. This money is used to debit your everyday losses if any. The original amount deposited is known as the initial margin and once the contract is ended or liquidated, the amount is refunded but the amount that is refundable is calculated by adding or subtracting any gains or losses respectively from the initial margin. The amount of this deposit is usually 5 to 10 percent of the futures contract and it changes daily according to the market fluctuation of the prices. Now the other term we mentioned earlier is the 'maintenance margin'. It is the lowest amount limit that an account can reach in the futures contract after which it needs to be replenished. This occurs when you are regularly facing losses in the contract and are required to make additional deposits to raise the margin amount to the initial amount. Here is an important advice. Always make sure you when the funds reach the lowest limit that is the 'maintenance margin', additional funds should be submitted immediately otherwise major losses could occur due to the liquidation of your position by the other party in order to cover up the losses incurred by them on your behalf.

The 'leverage' is another term that you may come across with during your hours at the futures market. It can be explained as a very small amount of initial margin that is used to enter into the futures contract of relatively large cash values of the commodities involved. As the futures market is highly risky, it is highly leveraged too. This can be considered as a contribution factor to great profits as well as great losses. Consider a price of a futures market to rise slightly. This profit will be large in comparison to the amount deposited as the initial margin. The same principle works the other way around too. A slight fall in the prices of the futures market will lead to greater losses in comparison to the initial margin amounts.

As mentioned earlier, the price discovery is the reason behind the setting up of contracts in the futures contract. These prices can only move up and down to the limited extent only and these minimums are set up by the futures exchanges which are known as 'ticks'. These price limits decide the amount up to which a contract can trade daily through the futures market. Try to understand this with an example – We have a futures contract whose price limit is set to Rs. 25. Now it is the yesterday's closing price to which the price limit amount will be added or subtracted to decide the upper and lower limit of the price movements in the futures contract. The upper boundary will be calculated by adding the price limit amount to the yesterday's closing price. If the closing price is Rs. 100 then the upper price limit will be Rs. 125. Similarly if we want to calculate the lower price boundary the same will be subtracted from the yesterday's closing price that in this case will be Rs. 75. The main purpose of applying price limits is to avoid any unfair advantages of the contract and this also ensure that it is not a single person that controls the market price of a specific commodity.

THE STRATEGIES

Let us move forward to building a strategy. Earlier we discussed two positions in the futures market – the long one and the short one. These positions are what make up a strategy. The participants in the futures market use up different strategy according to their position in the futures market to make profits from the rising and declining prices of the market. Now we have two options, one may decide to 'Go Long' and the other oppositely may choose to 'Go Short', entirely depending on his/her understanding and comfort zone of the futures market.

GOING LONG: As mentioned earlier, going long in the futures contract determines that the holder or the trader is making consent to buy and receive delivery of the underlying asset. The payment will be pre set. This means that an anticipated futures price increase will be the source of his income and profit. For example, a speculator buys a January contract of silver at Rs. 5000 per ounce. The no of ounces he agrees to buy is 100 turning the overall amount to be Rs. 5, 00,000. Now buying in October and setting the goals for January, he is actually getting into a long position. The speculator is anticipating the price of the silver to rise by the expiry date of his contract. The prices rise in December by Rs. 10 per ounce which will make Rs. 5010 per ounce to be the price of silver. The speculator decides to sell the contract wanting to get profits. For a total of 100 ounce the contract will now cost Rs. 5, 01,000. Thus the contract left a profit of Rs. 1000 for the trader. The speculator is on 100 percent profit. Undoubtedly the opposite of this will lead to 100 percent loss which will occur through the drop of prices by Rs. 10. Through the time of the contract if the account falls to the margin, the speculator will have to face major losses due to the respond to a number of margin calls.

GOING SHORT: Opposite to what a long going trader would do, the speculator going short is actually agreeing to sell and deliver the asset at a price mentioned in the contract. Therefore such a trader is making profit from the decline in the price values of the market. Hbbe works on the phenomenon of selling high and buying low which ultimately leaves him with a fair amount of profit. A speculator who is assuming the prices of oil to fall in the next coming months will consider it profitable to sell a contract today than later in the year. The current market prices are higher than the trader's speculation of the coming market situation leading to more profit now than later. This strategy actually takes advantage of a declining market situation. When the prices decline, the same trader would buy the same contract at the declined price which finally concludes into a profit statement.

It can be said that it depends all on your research of the futures market that will lead the results either into huge profits or huge gains.

The next we are going to discuss the spread trading strategy. It is considered as the most profitable and rather easy way to trade too with some professional skills in your hand. Certainly a volatile market is not a cup of tea of all. Some of us do need a sense of security while we trade. Spread trading can be considered as an option by such traders to protect themselves from the risk. The definition of spreads trading comes out to be the raise of profit from the discrepancy in the prices when a trader buys one commodity and sells another contract of the same commodity. So the capitalization comes from the price difference between the two futures contract while also hedging against the risk. The futures spread are quite infrequent though. There are different types of future spreads and also different ways to employ them.

- **INTER-COMMODITY FUTURES SPREAD:** These contracts are spread between different markets. These markets will be interpreted as one above the other irrespective of the increase or decrease in the price of the associated commodities. For example: a trader decides to work with two crops – corn and wheat. He speculates that the corn is going to have a higher demand than the wheat market, so he would decide to buy corn and sell wheat. He would not be bothered by the increase or decrease in the prices of these two crops but what would matter him will be the higher price of one crop over the other.

- **INTRA-COMMODITY CALENDER SPREAD:** It is the spread of same commodity in the same market but over different months of the calendar. For example: the corn can be spread as July corn and December corn. It can be either one of them – a long July corn and short December corn or a short July corn and long December Corn.

The spreads trading in futures market is known to be more lovable as well as reliable than trading from single long or short term positions. This technique is also known as pairs trading. It provides leverage and also helps in hedging risks in a systematic manner. When combined with risk management, cost effectiveness and margin efficiency, a futures spread trading can form a far superior strategy than a simple flat futures trading. When you are trading in future spreads, there is no stop running. As there are no stops involved, it can be considered as one of the purest forms of trading. Every spread can be seen as a hedge, so the risk factor is quite reduced. It is also known to lower the margin requirements which results in a greater efficiency in the use of your capital. With spreads trading, you can also trade in less liquid markets which lead to more opportunities altogether. There is always a greater possibility of winning than losing. Inverted markets are no longer a problem with the spreads trading. It is able to produce 10 times more return on margin than normal trading.

The 'futures trading' is not for everyone because it involves risk factors. So it is important to make sure about the amount of risk you are willing to undertake. You must be able to devote time, attention and research to an investment.

Chapter 3: UNDERSTANDING THE 'OPTIONS' AND PLANNING STRATEGIES

The Options are very dear to a sophisticated trader. It provides a handful of opportunities to those who are willing to work. They are very versatile and this property is what opens up major power sources linked to this trade. They allow you to fit into different situations according to the requirements and positions.

They can be manipulated to suit your needs. Therefore, it would not be a problem for options to be speculative as well as conservative to various extents as you desire. With this much of benefits availed, you cannot expect it to come without its costs. Being a complex security, they are hugely tricky as well as risky too. So always enter this market with your risk amount in hand and be ready to face a market based on speculations. One important condition to be successful in the options market is to know what you are doing. Being an amateur would be your first step towards huge losses. Do not enter it as an inexperienced trader. Do remember it is risky and you need to understand everything about it to produce profitable statements in your favor. Don not step into fear before learning because it is one of the most important parts of the world's largest corporations and you would not want to lose insight of such great opportunities in your life. You will need experience but eventually you will reach for it. Let us understand what the definition of an option holds in: It is defined as a contract between the seller and the buyer that gives the right to the buyer to buy or sell an underlying asset at a specific price on or before the expiry date. Now there is a difference between having the 'right' and being 'obliged' that forms the core of this contract. The buyer of the contract is not obliged to buy or sell the underlying asset but he has the right to. Hence, an options contract is a binding contract with defined terms and conditions. Consider this example, you want to buy a bike from the seller but the problem is you would not be able to come up with the amount of selling price required for the next couple of months. Now the seller can bind you in the option contract that would say that you can buy this bike in the next two months for a defined price. Now to set up this deal you will have to pay a certain amount that would be a short percentage of the original amount of the bike. Later, it is discovered that the bike is some early edition of the company as a result of which the price hiked to triple of its initial value. Now as the seller has made a contract with you, he is obliged to sell you the bike for the initial value of it. Thus it leaves you with a huge profit. But let us take another flip and say that the bike is just a normal one and not any early edition of the company but it is also useless in terms of average and machinery. So you drop the idea of buying it. As you are not obliged to buy it, you can easily leave the contract but still you will lose your contract binding amount given initially. We learned two very important points from the above example:

1. The first one is that the option contract is all about the 'right' and nothing about the 'obligation'. Although you will lose 100 percent of your money but you can skip up the expiry date after which the contract will no longer be retained. You will have a choice to buy or not to buy. That means you have 'options'.

2. An option is a contract that gets its value from the underlying asset. That is why it is a part of derivatives. The underlying asset can be a stock or an index.

We have two types of options: The first one is 'call' and the other one is 'put'

CALL: A call grants you the right to buy an underlying asset at a defined price and within a specific period of time that is before the expiry date. The buyer of call will always hope that the stock will increase before the end date of the contract. It can be compared to a long position in the stock market.

PUT: A put grants you the right to sell an underlying asset at a defined price and within a specific period of time that is before the expiry date. The buyer of put will always hope that the price of the stock falls before the end date of the contract. It can be compared to a short position in the stock market. We have four different but interlinked kinds of participants in the options. These are:

1. Buyers of a call
2. Sellers of a call
3. Buyers of a put
4. Sellers of a put

The sellers are known as the 'writers' whereas the buyers are known as the 'holders'. Another important difference between the two lies in the fact that the call holders as well as put holders are not constrained to buy or sell. They have the right to choose and it is totally up to them to exercise it or not. Opposite to this the call writers as well as the put writers constrained to buy and sell. This option is riskier than the buying option.

Like every other discipline, the terminology needs to be cleared to develop an understanding of the whole subject. Let us get into it first:

- Strike Price: It is the price mentioned in the options contract. It is sometimes also known as the exercise price.

- American options: These options can be practiced up to the expiration date of the contract.

- European options: these options can be practiced only on the expiration date and not before it. In India, you will usually see European style settlement.

  *** The American and European options have nothing to do with the geographical location and they should be interpreted by definition.

- In-the-money option: In call options if the share price is over the strike price it will be referred to as in- the-money option. Similarly for a put option if the share price is below the strike price then it will be referred to as in-the-money potion.

- At-the-money: It is applied to an option when the spot price is equal to the strike price.

- Out-of-the money option: It is referred to an option when the spot price is below the strike price.

- Intrinsic value: The amount by which the option is maintained in a state of in-the-money is considered as the intrinsic value of the contract.

- Premium: It is referred to as the total price of an option.

- Time value: it is referred to as the amount of remaining time calculated from the expiration date. The difference between the premium of an option and its intrinsic value is the time value.

Why do we have to use options? There are two reasons of its success in the market – the first one is speculation and the second one is hedging. When we talk about speculation, it is nothing more than its definition. You are basically betting on the movement of a stock price. With options it does not matter if the market is heading upwards or downwards, you can make profits either way. Sideways is also an opportunity to make money in the options market. You can make huge profits or you can straight push yourself towards huge losses. That is why they are known to a risky endeavor. So here it is really important to be perfect in terms o selection of an option and correct in terms of determining the direction, magnitude and timing of its movement. Prediction is the only key you have and you cannot lose hold of it. And here when we say prediction it is not guessing but it is a step based on research and data. Hedging is another way to ensure your profits in the option strategies are very useful when large institutions are involved but with correct application they can also be useful to Individuals even during the odds. It basically restricts your downward movements.

We generally stick to the definition of options which states that option is the right and not an obligation to buy or sell a stock. While this is undoubtedly true but majorly these options are not actually exercised. Most of them are traded and the others expire which leaves no value to an option.

THE STRATEGIES:

1. The long call: The Bullish nature of the stocks can be very attractive to the aggressive investors. The long call is a very effective way to gain profits from the upwards potential of a market with very limited risk on the downside. Here you are buying a call and this idea has a very simple phenomenon behind it. When you buy call it directly indicates that you are bullish. You are hereby speculating the rise in the prices of an underlying asset. The risk is very much limited to just the premium and maximum loss can only occur if the market is expired at or below the strike price of the option.

Example: An investor is bullish and decides to buy a call at the strike price of Rs.3000 at a premium of Rs. 25. Suppose the market price is Rs. 2500. Now if the market price rises above Rs. 3025 (Strike price + premium), the investor will make a net profit after deducting the premium amount too. Another case scenario would be if the market price falls below the strike amount that is Rs. 3000. The investor will end up facing maximum loss of the premium and the option will expire worthlessly.

This strategy helps in limiting the risk of the downside movement to the extent of just the paid premium. Thus it reduces any major losses to the market. Moreover, this method is the simplest way to make money out of the upwards movement of the market. It is a quick and easy way to get into the options if you are rather sure of your belief of the uphill market movements in the near future.

2. The short call: It is opposite of the long call strategy. It is employed through the bearish sentiments and the investor sells the call options. Unlike the long call, an investor working with a short call is expecting the prices to fall in the near future. This position is more about limited profits and higher losses. It is easy in terms of execution but the seller is exposed to unlimited risk too.

Selling a call option is the exact opposite of buying the call option. The reward or the profits are very much limited to the amount of premium where as the risks are unlimited.

Example: An investor is bearish and decides to sell a call option at the strike price of Rs.3000 at a premium of Rs. 25. Suppose the market price is Rs.3050. Now if the market price stays same or below as Rs. 3000 (Strike price), the call option will not be processed by the buyer of the call and the seller of the call would be able to retain the entire benefit of the premium amount.

This strategy is usually employed when the aggressive investor is sure of the price falls of the market. Being a risky endeavor, it can cause in the loss of significant amount of money due to a drastic fall in the prices of the stock below the strike price.

3. The Synthetic Long Call – Buy stock, Buy put: This strategy is quite helpful to those who do not want to get stuck in the market. You buy a stock because you felt bullish about it. Now what if the sentiments of the market get on the opposite road? You would wish to have secured yourself of the price fall. This is when you buy a put. It gives you the right to sell the stock at the strike price of it. Now the strike price can either be exactly the initial buying price or can be slightly below it. If the situations go as you speculated them to, then the benefit has nowhere to run. It is all yours in its full action. The losses are very limited and the chances of winning are high. Even if you lose, it will be fairly less amount as compared to other plain losses as you will always be able to get the strike price of the option. This is because the 'put' stops your further losses. The profit is unlimited. Through this strategy you aim at holding a stock and producing profits out of it but at the same time also ensuring the limited risk situation. It allows you to take complete advantage of the price movements. You can understand as an ownership of a stock with lesser risks. This method is generally known to be conservatively bullish.

Example: An investor is bullish about some stock which he buys at the current market price of Rs. 4000. He is afraid of the downwards movement of the market. To protect against this he buys a put option with a strike price of Rs. 3900 with a premium amount of Rs. 100. The breakeven point of this stock is thus Rs. 4100.

This is a comparatively low risk strategy. It limits the loss in while the intensity of profits remains unlimited.

4. The long put: as the name suggest, it is totally opposite of buying a call. The bearish sentiments are the main driving force behind adopting this strategy. It gives the right to sell a stock at a specified price. This limit the risk associated with normal selling of the stocks. The long put strategy allows you to take that advantage of the downwards movement of a market. The risk is also limited to the premium amount paid and the maximum loss is faced when the stock expires at or below the strike price. The profit is unlimited Example: the investor is speculating the market to be bearish. So he buys a put option whose strike price is Rs 3000 with the premium payment of Rs. 100. The market price is Rs. 3500. If the market price heads below Rs. 3400, the investor will make a profit after exercising the option. Just in case the market price rises, the investor will face a loss but to a maximum extent of premium amount.

5. **Short put:** it is already known that selling a put is different from buying a put. You will buy a put in bearish sentiments while sell it in bullish sentiments. An investor who sells a put gets a premium amount from the buyer. You have now sold someone the right to sell you the stock at the strike price. This position will be profitable by the amount of premium for a seller if the stock price goes beyond the strike price. This is because the buyer will not exercise his right and the premium amount will be all left for the put seller. But the opposite of this situation is also true. If the stock price goes below the strike price by going over the amount of premium, the put seller will lose money. The loss is unlimited. The main motive behind planning this strategy is to make short

term income as the reward is limited to the premium amount only.

Example: an investor is bullish and decides to sell a put option with a strike price of Rs. 3000 with a premium payment of Rs 50. The market price is at Rs. 3100. If the market stays above Rs. 3000, the put buyer would not exercise his right and the seller will retain the benefits of the premium amount. But if the market goes other way around and the prices fall below Rs. 3000, the put seller will have to lose his money. The loss is unlimited and depends upon the fall mainly.

This strategy can be source of regular income in rage bound markets. Hence it can be considered as an income generating strategy.

Chapter 4: THE DIFFERENCE

The futures and options are both a part of derivatives but they are different from each other. The key fundamental difference is on the basis of the obligations they put on their participants. An option gives the right and does not impose obligations to buy or sell the underlying asset whereas a futures contract imposes an obligation on the buyer to purchase a certain asset. Similarly under a futures contract, the seller is also obliged to sell as well as deliver the underlying asset.

Another difference is in the way of entry into these two. A futures contract does not imply any upfront costs of entering into the market. But in the options market it is required to pay a certain amount of payment which is known as the premium. This upfront cost can be understood as the cost of getting the privilege of non-obligated contract. This is not the case in the futures market. The premium amount is the maximum amount of money that a buyer can lose while dealing in options.

Another difference that defines the options and futures lies in the size of the underlying asset. In futures contract, the underlying is large and being an obligatory trade position it is highly risky for an inexperienced and amateur trader or investor.

One difference also is the way these two receive their gains. The gains in the futures are a three way divergence. The first one is to exercise the option when it is in-the money. The second one is to trade through the market and take opposite positions. The last one is to collect the difference of the market price of the asset and the strike price mentioned in the contract. While when we take futures into deal, the positions are daily updated into your account at the end of every trading day.

The benefits: The most important benefit of trading in futures and options is that you have the chances of transferring your risks to someone who is willing to work through them. And noteworthy is that you can make profits with minimum amounts of risk money. Transaction cost is also low, so it is also a positive factor. The liquidity is the most important characteristic of both futures and options trade. It enables price discovery in the market. These are a leading group of trade essentials that are very fair economic indicators. You can basically trade the whole stock market using these two techniques.

It is usually assumed that the futures and options market is always riskier than other investment methods but this can never be true for all the times. A proper risk management strategy always goes a long way in providing great benefits out of the stock market. This fact has its roots in the understanding the concept of leverage and hedging. While it is also true you should never step into the futures and options market without enough risk funds in your hand, it can also be said that this venture is undoubtedly a great way to earn profits and drawing limit lines to the risk factors of the stock market.

DISCLAIMER AND/OR LEGAL NOTICES:

Every effort has been made to accurately represent this book and its potential. Results vary with every individual, and your results may or may not be different from those depicted. No promises, guarantees or warranties, whether stated or implied, have been made that you will produce any specific result from this book. Your efforts are individual and unique, and may vary from those shown. Your success depends on your efforts, background and motivation. The material in this publication is provided for educational and informational purposes only and is not intended as financial advice. The information contained in this book should not be used as an investment advice. Always consult a professional financial advisor before investing. Use of the programs, advice, and information contained in this book is at the sole choice and risk of the reader.

Printed in Great Britain
by Amazon